# ILLUSTRATED BY
# CHUCK WHELON

## WRITTEN BY SOPHIE SCHREY

### DESIGNED BY ANGIE ALLISON AND ZOE BRADLEY

WHERE'S THE PENGUIN?

Buster Books

# Meet The Family

A clever family of penguins has escaped from a city zoo. They are on a mission to get back to their real home in Antarctica. Along the way, the penguins stop off at lots of exciting places, and have all kinds of fun.

Join the feathered family on their journey, and pick out all ten penguins in every picture. Find the answers plus extra things to spot at the back of the book.

# Penguin Profiles

# Escape From The Zoo!

The penguins were bored with life at the zoo, so they have escaped from their enclosure. They are enjoying their new-found freedom, completely unaware of the chaos they have created around them.

Spike loves skateboarding and Muffy cannot believe that ice in cones tastes so good.

Can you pick out all ten penguins?

# Time To Shop

The first stop for the penguins is a shopping mall to buy supplies for their journey. Snowflake is in heaven. With so many pretty things to buy, she doesn't know where to begin.

Dot is fascinated with the strange moving stairs and Spike has discovered that the shiny floors make a great surface for sliding on. Watch out!

Can you pick out all ten penguins?

# Fancy-Dress Fun

The penguins stumble upon a birthday celebration. Amelia thinks the monkeys at the zoo seemed calm in comparison to the kids at this party.

Hugo heads straight for the party food to nibble on the sandwiches, while Arnie stretches his wings and gets ready for a game of tug-of-war.

Can you pick out all ten penguins?

# Haunted House

Arnie thought he had found the family a quiet place to rest their wings for the night. Little did he know that after dark there would be a spooky party in the house with very peculiar guests.

The penguins soon realize these people are NOT wearing fancy dress and they dive for cover. Spike, however, thinks these ghosts, ghouls, witches and weird monsters are the coolest thing ever.

Can you pick out all ten penguins?

# By The Lake

After the excitement of the past few days, the lake is the perfect place for the penguins to lie back and relax in the sunshine.

There's plenty to keep the young ones entertained. Pee-Wee can't stop playing in the sand, and Dot is having a fantastic time splashing around and trying out the different water sports.

Can you pick out all ten penguins?

# Go-Karting

It's Amelia's birthday today, and the penguins were surprised when she said that she wanted to try her wings at go-karting. Spike is thrilled. He can't wait to get behind the wheel for some high-speed fun.

The crowd is going crazy with excitement as the cars zoom around the track. It's going to be a close race to the finish line ... go, go, go!

Can you pick out all ten penguins?

# Feeding Time

Brian has decided to treat the family to a fancy meal this evening and he's picked the best restaurant in town.

Hugo can't resist getting his beak into all of the tasty dishes. There are so many different foods to try and he wants to make sure that he leaves plenty of room for cake. Yummy!

Can you pick out all ten penguins?

# At The Carnival

The penguins have landed at a carnival parade, and they are ready to party. Snowflake is so excited – the music, the dancing and the bright costumes are so magical.

Amelia wants to waddle her way onto a float, while Muffy has the giggles. She has spotted Topper in the middle of the action, shaking his tail feathers.

Can you pick out all ten penguins?

# In The Desert

Amelia is thrilled that the penguin family has arrived in a desert town on market day. The streets are buzzing and there are so many delicious things to smell and interesting things to look at.

It's too hot for some members of the family, but for Muffy the temperature is just right. She loves the feel of the sun on her feathers.

Can you pick out all ten penguins?

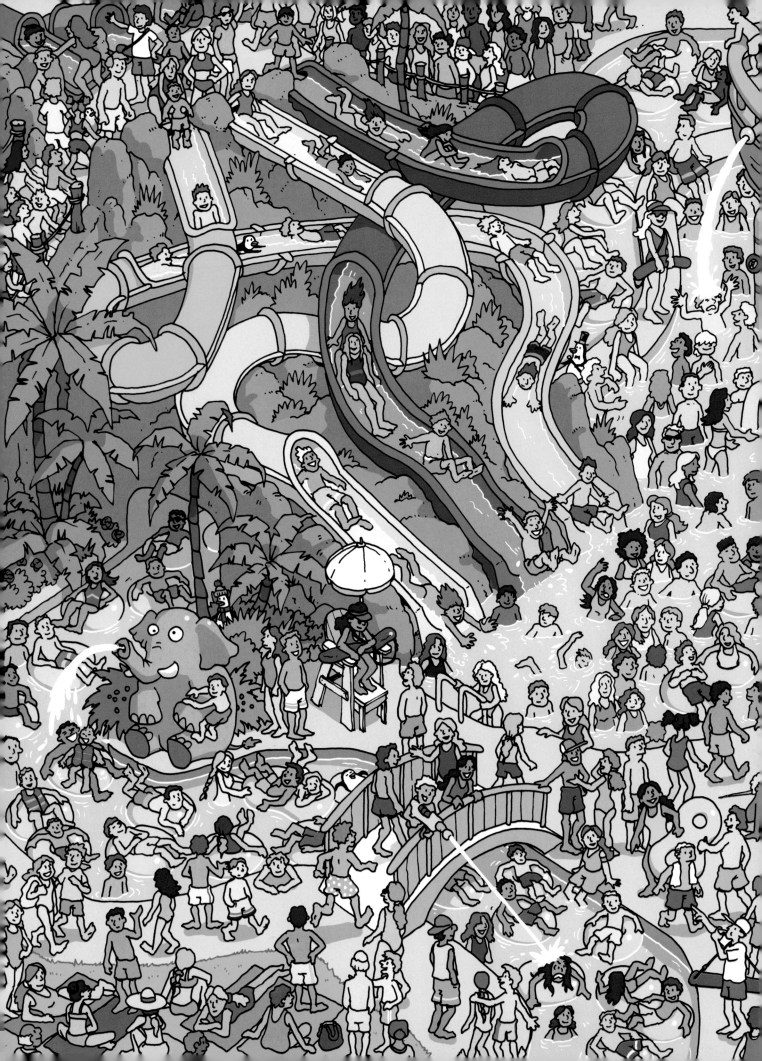

# Making A Splash

Ever since Pee-Wee and Snowflake spotted the bright wiggly slides in the distance, they've been pestering Amelia to let them go to the water park.

Now the whole family is enjoying splashing around. Arnie is busy organizing fun games for everyone, while Brian is trying to pluck up the courage to fight his fear of heights and go down the giant flume.

Can you pick out all ten penguins?

# A Grand Orchestra

Topper is a huge fan of classical music and loved listening to it on the radio back at the zoo. To watch a real orchestra in concert is a dream come true for him.

Amelia is caught up in the beauty of the music, but Snowflake thinks it sounds like a lot of horrible noise. She's far more interested in looking at all the amazing outfits in the audience.

Can you pick out all ten penguins?

# Bowling Fun!

It's been raining all day so the penguins have stopped for a while to shelter inside a busy bowling alley.

Arnie has jumped straight in, bowling with the heaviest ball. He is in a competition with Topper to see who can get the most strikes in a row. The adult penguins are going to grab a drink and plan the final route for their journey back home.

Can you pick out all ten penguins?

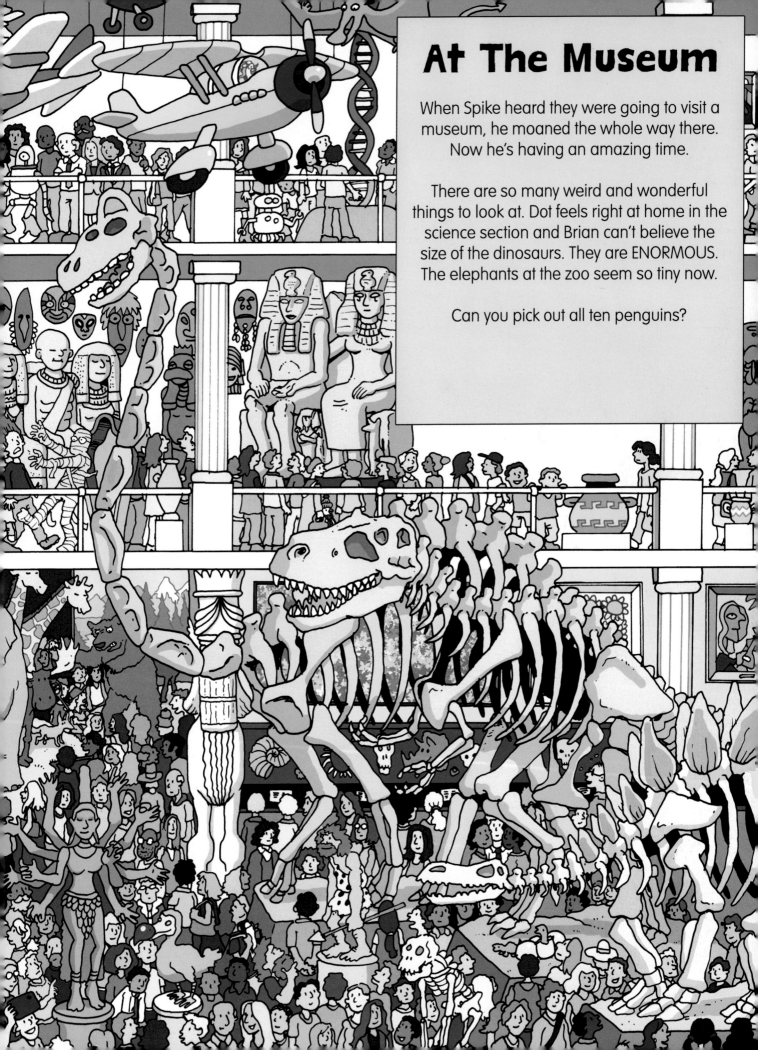

# At The Museum

When Spike heard they were going to visit a museum, he moaned the whole way there. Now he's having an amazing time.

There are so many weird and wonderful things to look at. Dot feels right at home in the science section and Brian can't believe the size of the dinosaurs. They are ENORMOUS. The elephants at the zoo seem so tiny now.

Can you pick out all ten penguins?

# Under The Sea

Hugo was delighted when he managed to hitch the family a ride on a big ship. But then the captain caught him eating the crew's fish soup, and the penguins had to dive overboard and escape.

The tropical waters are very different from what they remember of Antarctica. Pee-Wee is mesmerized by the beautiful shoals of fish, while Amelia is trying to stay as far away from the sharks as possible. Eeek!

Can you pick out all ten penguins?

# Sky High

It's an exciting day for the penguins as they finally discover what it feels like to fly. Muffy is finding it all a bit overwhelming. The sky seems a very busy place to be, and she prefers to be underwater where it is calm.

For Spike it is without a doubt the coolest thing he's ever done. He loves zooming, dipping and dodging his way around the flying objects.

Can you pick out all ten penguins?

# Lost In Space

Brian's map reading has got the penguin family a little lost. He's missed Antarctica, their final destination, and managed to navigate the family into space.

Dot thought humans looked weird, but these alien creatures are even stranger, and so slimy. Snowflake is speechless and for once she is not enjoying the number of eyes on her. She thinks the stars are beautiful though, and the alien pets are kind of cute.

Can you pick out all ten penguins?

PENGUIN SPOTTER TOURS

# Home Sweet Home

After an incredible journey, the penguins have arrived back in Antarctica and they are VERY happy to be home. They have brought plenty of gifts for their friends and family to share.

Pee-Wee is delighted that she has finally got penguins her own age to play with, and Topper is bursting to tell everyone stories about their adventures.

Can you pick out all ten penguins in the family?

# Answers

I'm also in every picture, trying to catch those naughty penguins. Can you spot me?

## Extra Things To Spot

Six children wearing animal masks ☑

A monkey reading a newspaper ☑

A man eating an apple ☑

A cheeky raccoon ☐

A woman taking a photograph ☐

**Escape From The Zoo!**

**Time To Shop**

## Extra Things To Spot

A child holding a teddy bear ☐

A security guard catching a thief ☐

A man playing the guitar ☐

A girl on her father's shoulders ☐

Someone wearing headphones ☐

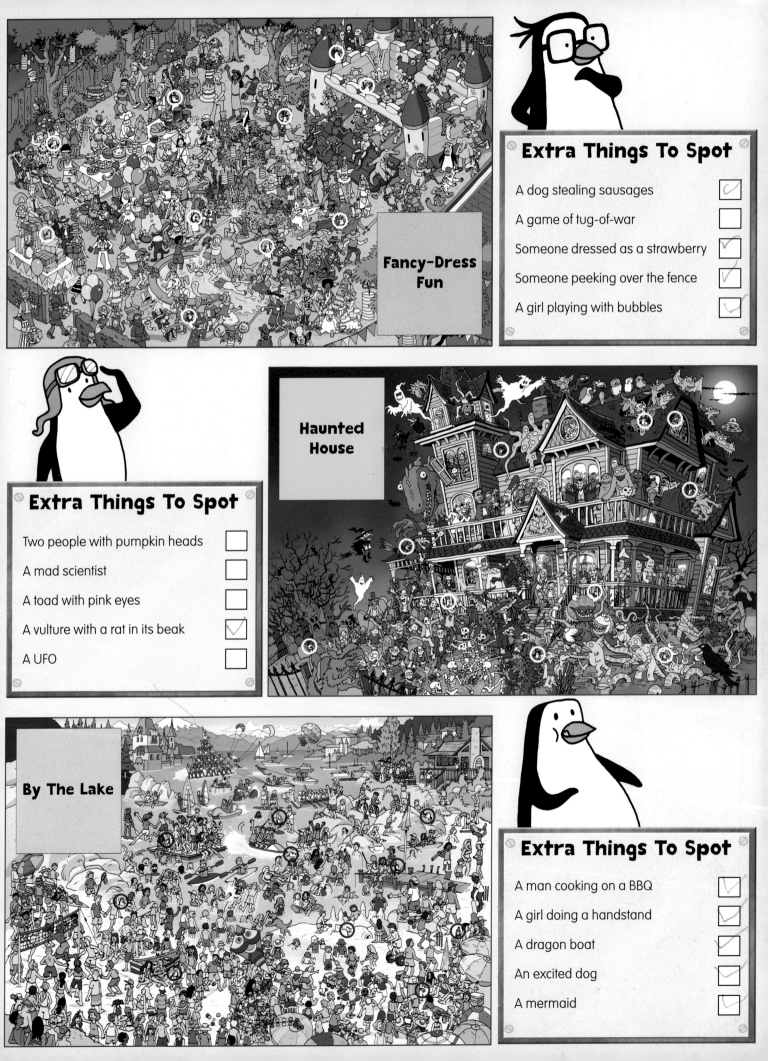

**Fancy-Dress Fun**

## Extra Things To Spot

| | |
|---|---|
| A dog stealing sausages | ☑ |
| A game of tug-of-war | ☐ |
| Someone dressed as a strawberry | ☑ |
| Someone peeking over the fence | ☑ |
| A girl playing with bubbles | ☑ |

**Haunted House**

## Extra Things To Spot

| | |
|---|---|
| Two people with pumpkin heads | ☐ |
| A mad scientist | ☐ |
| A toad with pink eyes | ☐ |
| A vulture with a rat in its beak | ☑ |
| A UFO | ☐ |

**By The Lake**

## Extra Things To Spot

| | |
|---|---|
| A man cooking on a BBQ | ☑ |
| A girl doing a handstand | ☑ |
| A dragon boat | ☑ |
| An excited dog | ☑ |
| A mermaid | ☑ |

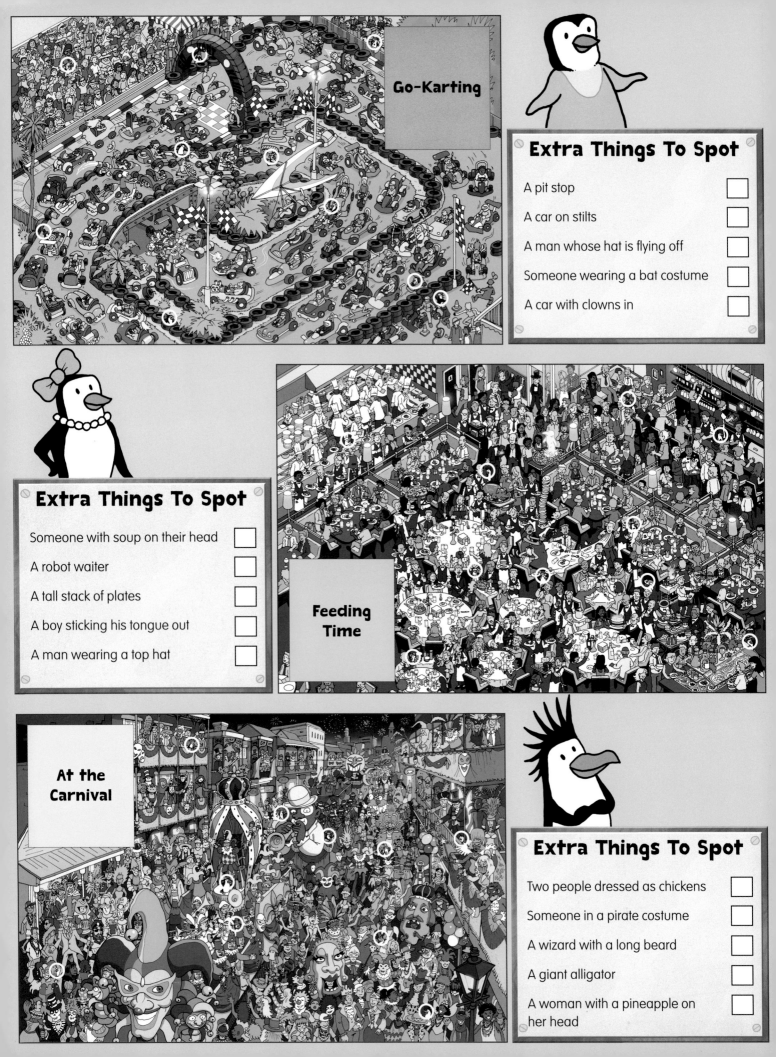

Go-Karting

## Extra Things To Spot

A pit stop ☐

A car on stilts ☐

A man whose hat is flying off ☐

Someone wearing a bat costume ☐

A car with clowns in ☐

## Extra Things To Spot

Someone with soup on their head ☐

A robot waiter ☐

A tall stack of plates ☐

A boy sticking his tongue out ☐

A man wearing a top hat ☐

Feeding Time

At the Carnival

## Extra Things To Spot

Two people dressed as chickens ☐

Someone in a pirate costume ☐

A wizard with a long beard ☐

A giant alligator ☐

A woman with a pineapple on her head ☐

In The Desert

**Extra Things To Spot**

A snake charmer ☐

Someone falling off a camel ☐

A tourist with a video camera ☐

A man riding a donkey ☐

Someone inside a giant pot ☐

**Extra Things To Spot**

A kid squirting a water pistol ☐

Three lifeguards with whistles ☐

A woman in a stripey bikini ☐

A man with spotty trunks ☐

A boy wearing a snorkel and mask ☐

Making A Splash

A Grand Orchestra

**Extra Things To Spot**

A woman knitting ☐

Someone with binoculars ☐

A musician wearing a sombrero ☐

A girl reading a book ☐

A man eating popcorn ☐

**Bowling Fun!**

## Extra Things To Spot

A man wearing a crown ☐

A man with a green mohawk ☐

A woman on a dance machine ☐

A man with a pink beard ☐

Someone bowling through their legs ☐

## Extra Things To Spot

A walking mummy ☐

Two hatching dinosaurs ☐

A dodo ☐

An astronaut ☐

A grizzly bear ☐

**At The Museum**

**Under The Sea**

## Extra Things To Spot

An anchor ☐

Three mermaids ☐

A whale ☐

A giant sea snail ☐

A treasure chest ☐

## Sky High

## Lost In Space

## Home Sweet Home

### A Final Challenge

The family has given their penguin friends gifts they've collected from all of the places they've visited. Can you work out which scenes each of the different objects have come from? Look back through the book to help you.